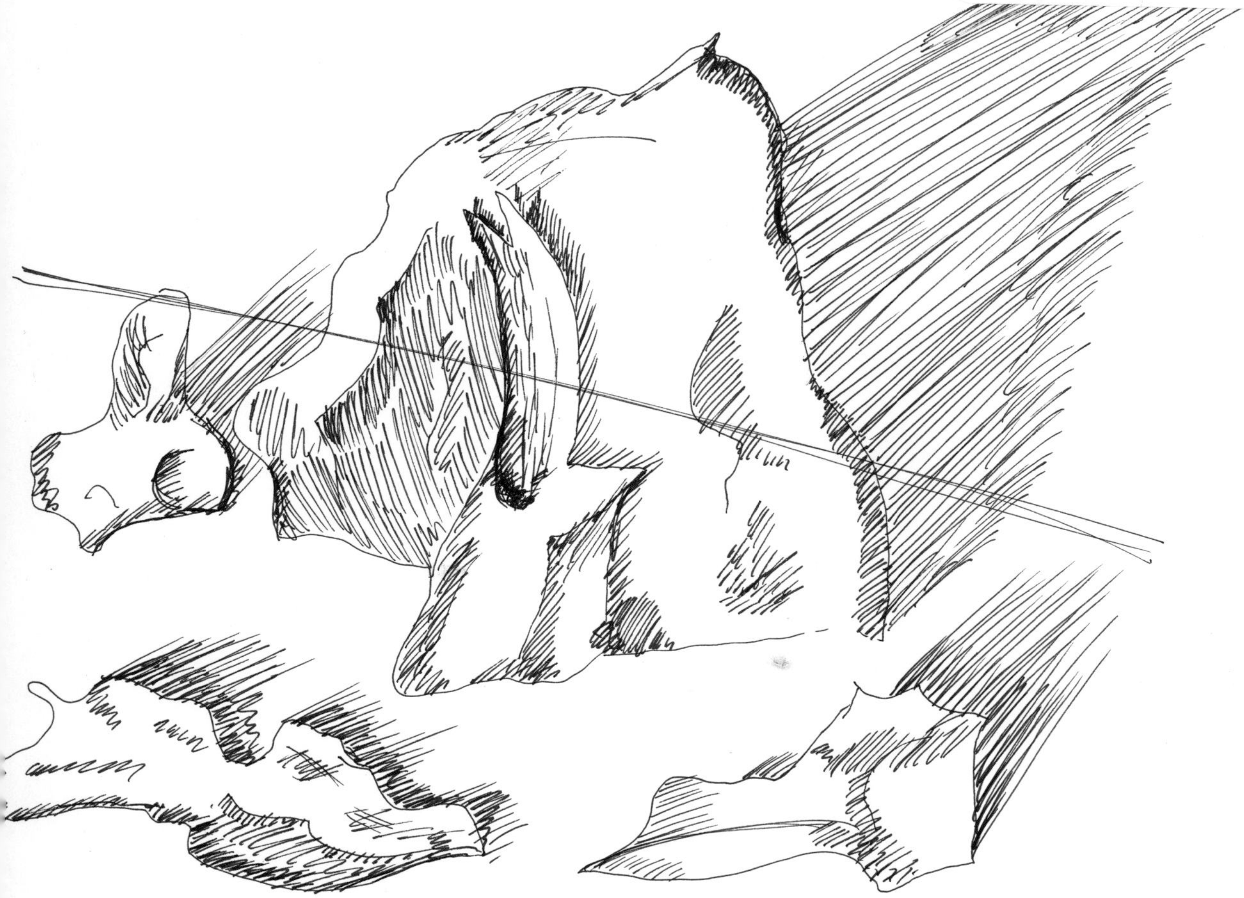

In any given scene, or object, once you control its
lines, you control it . . . Line implies mastery.
WYNDHAM LEWIS

Still Life

The timeless genre of still-life art—non-living objects arranged in a specific way to create meaning or a visual effect—can speak volumes about their invisible owner, or be imbued with symbolism, poignancy, or unadulterated joy by the artist depicting them. Still-life artwork began to grow in popularity during the 1600s, as European artists began exploring the genre as a way to communicate messages through their art, such as imminent mortality or the celebration of life through food, objects, and bountiful floral configurations. Collectors and connoisseurs purchased them because of their realism, visual appeal, and relevance to their own lives; poets praised the wonders of the art form to transcend the seasons and the passing of time.

David Hockney (b.1937) said that "how you depict something is a formal problem . . . there's no solution to it. There are a thousand ways you can go about it." And this is what makes drawing appealing—you can tackle it any way that you want, using your own experiences and choosing still-life subjects that you particularly like to make your work individual to you. A final drawing is an end in itself, but the skills gained from drawing are also essential basics for all visual art. This sketchbook is part of a series to help develop your drawing skills across a range of subjects, and in this book we include a selection of still-life drawings that cover a range of traditions and media to copy from and be inspired by. These are accompanied by thoughts from commentators and the artists themselves, and there is also a general information section included on materials and techniques for the beginner.

As well as visual delights, still-life drawing is of particular appeal as you can easily arrange the composition, lighting, and items exactly to your requirements. The object cannot move or twitch like a live model; the lighting can be controlled unlike the evanescent light of a shifting landscape. You don't have to wait until you have the time to draw a complete still-life scene; preparatory sketches, practice exercises, or even a few scribbles will go a long way to sharpening your observation skills, and the practice of keeping a sketchbook will provide a significant record of your processes, experimentations, and thoughts.

The examples of still lifes set by the great artists in this sketchbook will help you discover new skills, from understanding composition, form, and perspective to using color and rendering light, shade, and texture. But the ultimate aim of this book is to inspire you to find exquisiteness and potency in the objects available to you. Still lifes can remind us of how much beauty the world has to offer, and with practice you can turn everyday objects into beautiful drawings full of meaning, or take subjects important to you and feel that you can do them justice in your work.

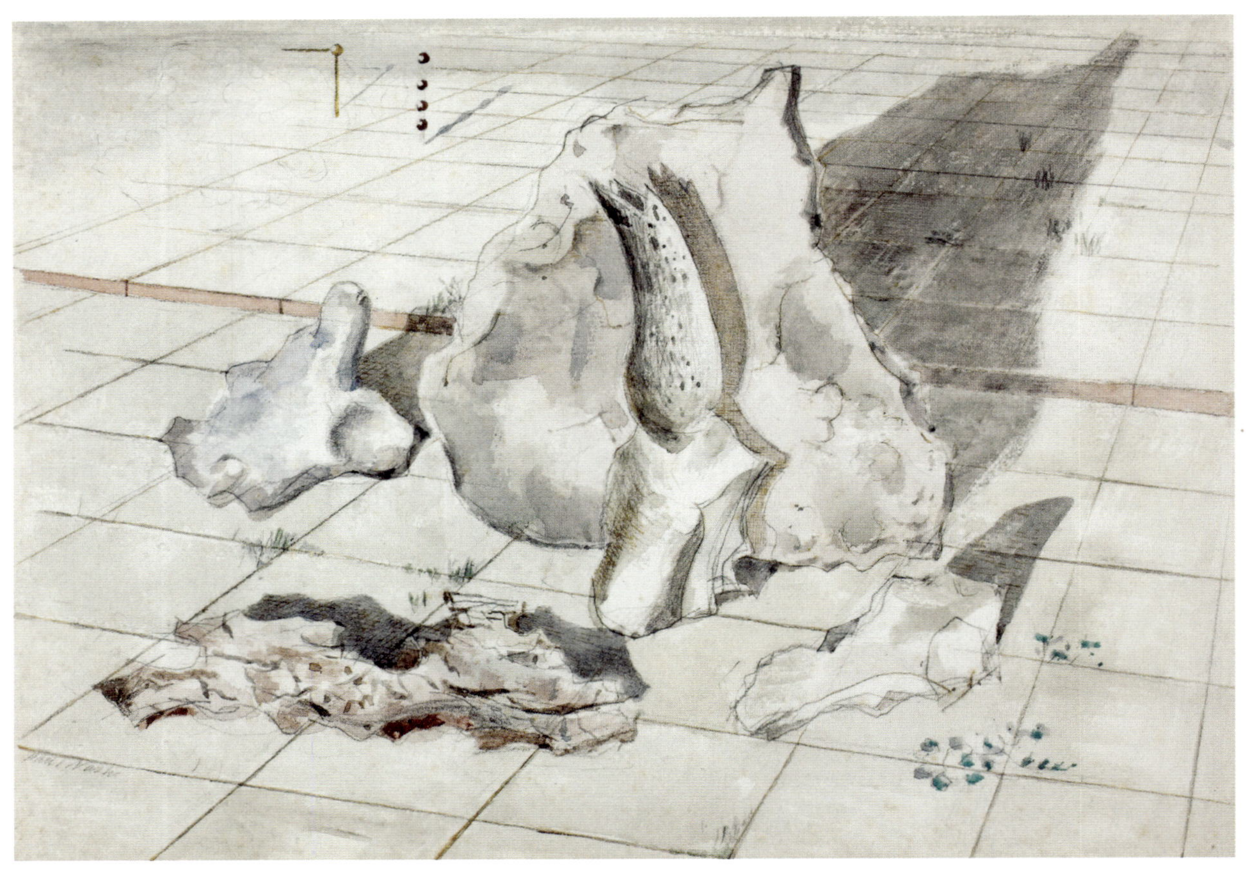

Paul Nash
(1889–1946)
STUDY FOR
LANDSCAPE
OF BLEACHED
OBJECTS
1934
Watercolor and
pencil on paper
Daniel Katz Gallery, London

Édouard Manet
(1832–1883)
TWO APPLES
1880
Watercolor over
graphite on wove paper
*National Gallery of Art,
Washington. Collection of
Mr. and Mrs. Paul Mellon*

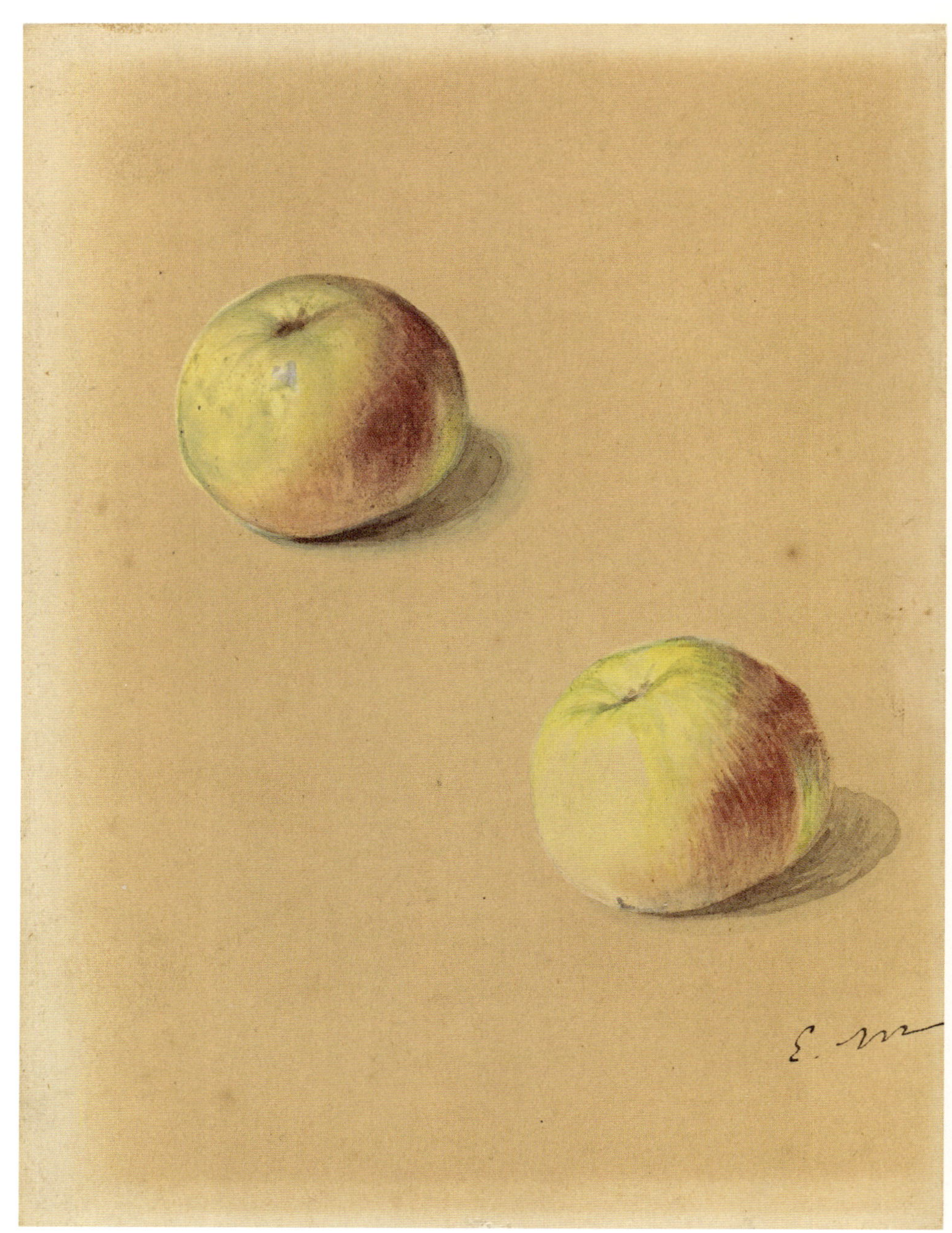

*Fruits . . . like having their portrait painted. They seem to sit there
and ask your forgiveness for fading . . . They come with all their
scents, they speak of the fields they have left, the rain which has
nourished them, the daybreaks they have seen.*

PAUL CÉZANNE

The immutability of a still-life arrangement is a gift
for any artist. Consider Cézanne's frustration at the
moving model: "You wretch! You've spoiled the pose.
Do I have to tell you again you must sit like an apple?
Does an apple move?"

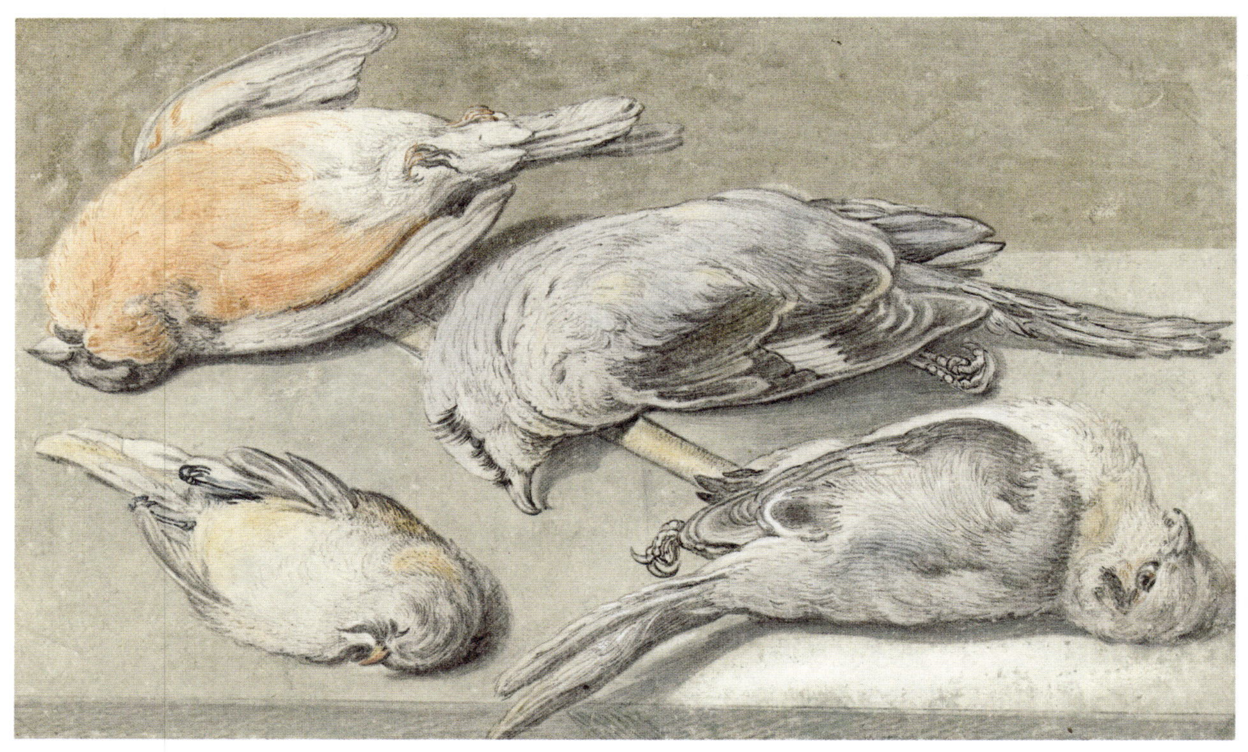

Elias Vonck
(c.1605–1652)
STILL LIFE WITH
FOUR DEAD BIRDS
C.1640–1652
Deck paint, watercolor
paint, and chalk on paper
Rijksmuseum, Amsterdam

In the seventeenth century, there was an entire genre of art
dedicated to depictions of dead birds and other game animals.
The advantage of the subjects were that they didn't move,
and so compared to live subjects, were a lot easier to draw.

Consider how you might extend the genre of drawing dead animals to sketching a sleeping pet instead. It will be similarly easy to draw your relatively motionless subject and you will achieve a serene or perhaps eerie effect as they appear frozen in time.

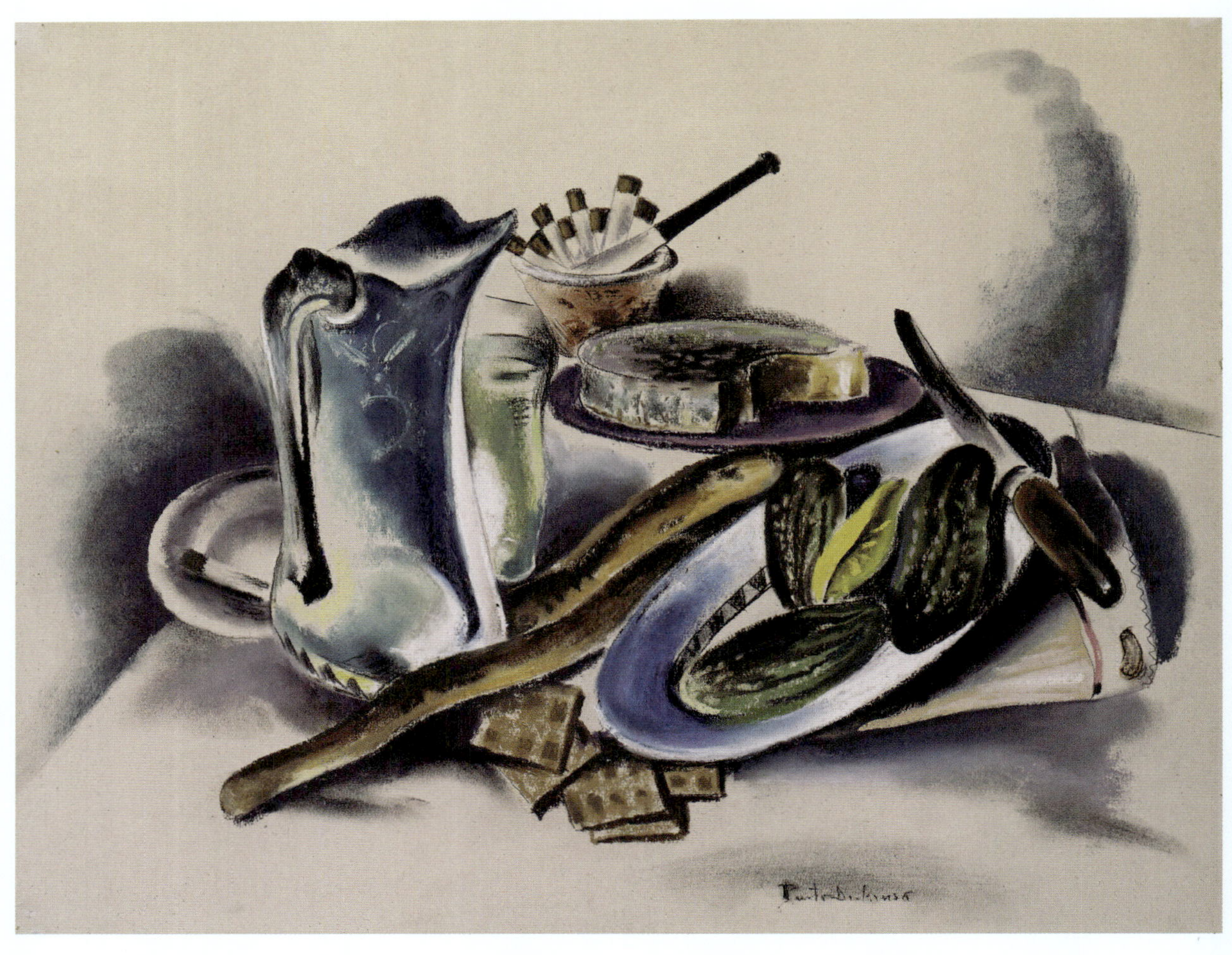

Preston Dickinson
(1889—1930)
STILL LIFE
C.1930
Pastel on paper,
mounted on cardboard
*The Metropolitan Museum
of Art, New York. The Lesley
and Emma Sheafer Collection,
Bequest of Emma A. Sheafer,
1973/Scala, Florence*

Known as "Immaculate" and "modern classicist," Dickinson
was particularly concerned with precise lines and industrial
subjects. Try to emulate his expressive use of color and
composition by adopting a wide-ranging palette of pastels
and including jagged angles in your work.

Select your composition carefully—consider what elements
about the objects fascinate you: the colors, shapes, textures,
and what whole image you can make from them.

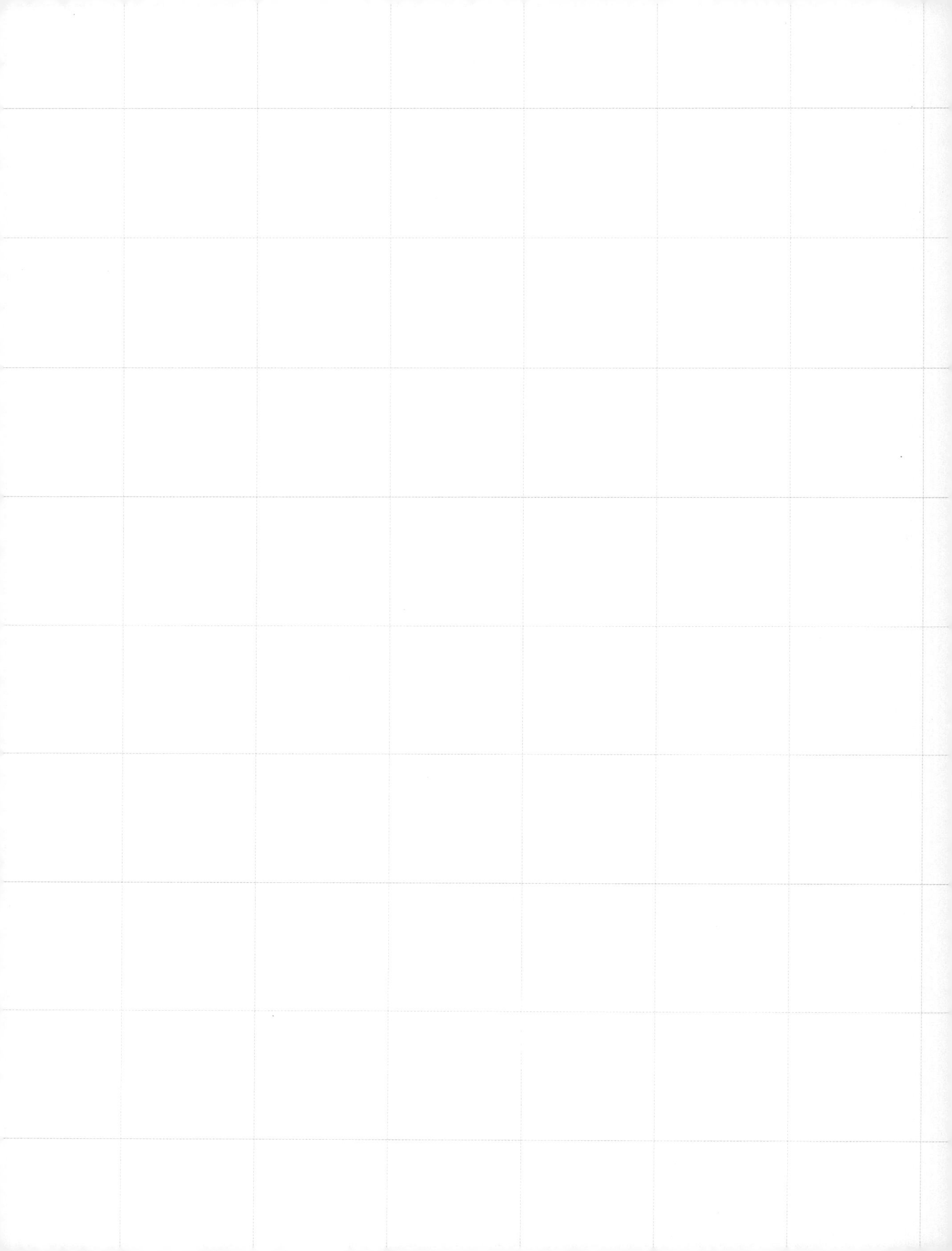

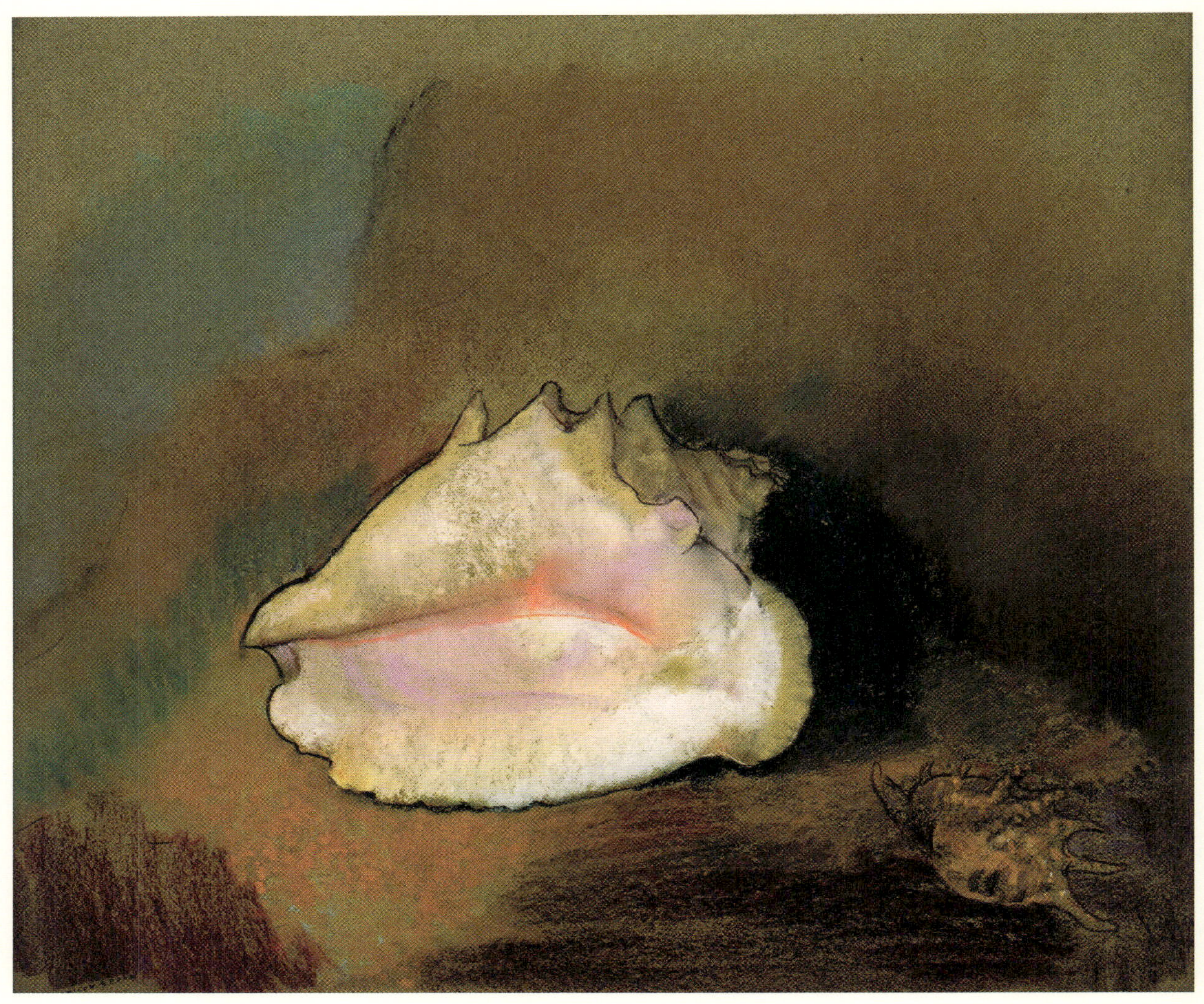

Odilon Redon
(1840–1916)
COQUILLAGE
(SHELL)
1912
Pastel on paper
Musée d'Orsay, Paris.
Gift of Suzanne und Arï
Redon, 1982/akg-images

Sketching is almost everything. It is the painter's identity, his style, his conviction, and then color is just a gift to the drawing.
FERNANDO BOTERO

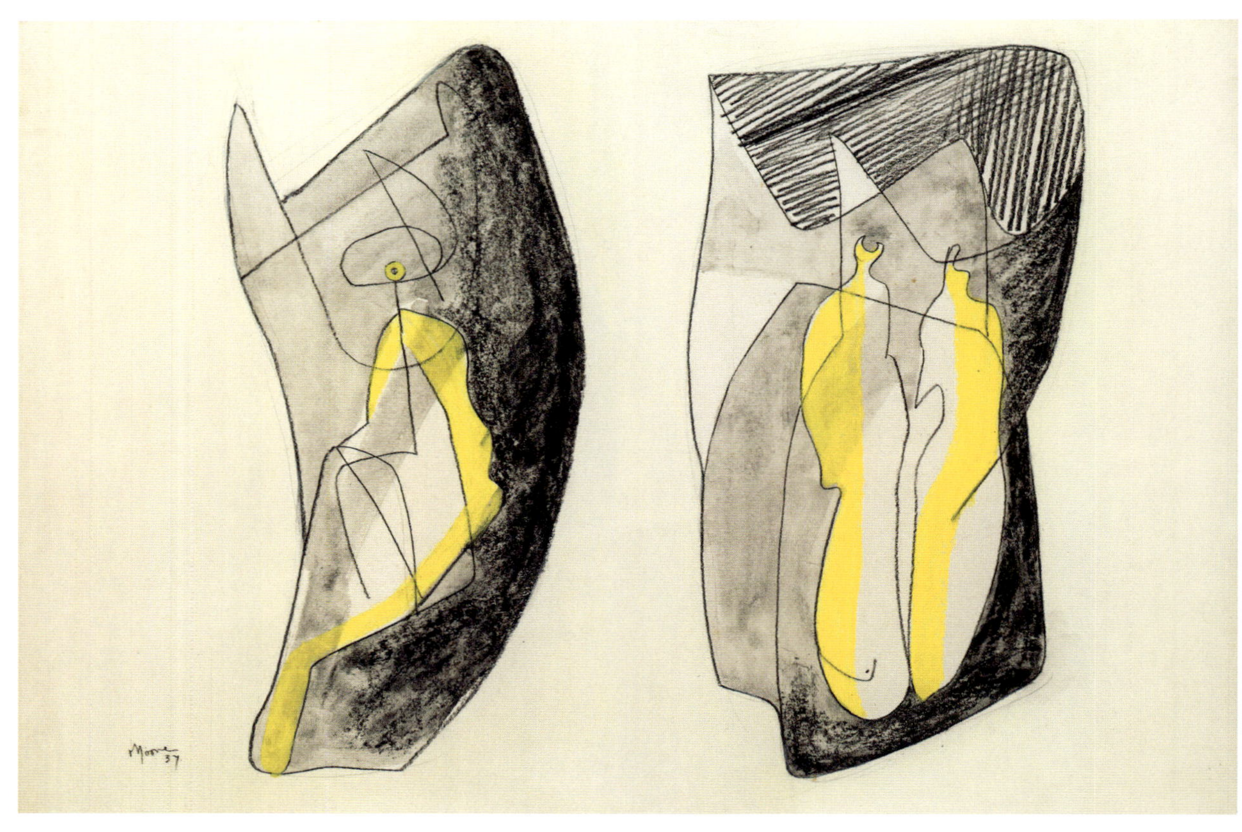

Henry Moore
(1898–1986)
DRAWING FOR
SCULPTURE:
TWO FORMS
1937
Pencil, charcoal,
chalk, gray wash,
crayon, and gouache
Private Collection/
photo Bonhams, London/
Bridgeman Images.
Reproduced by permission of
The Henry Moore Foundation

Moore would often take walks looking for inspiration in
natural subjects such as shells, pebbles, and pieces of
wood. He used his drawings to experiment and develop
his artworks of objects he found from the natural world,
to find the best variations of forms and designs.

Closely observe natural forms; focus on the minutiae
of ridged structures, regular and irregular patterns,
and textured surfaces to give life to objects.

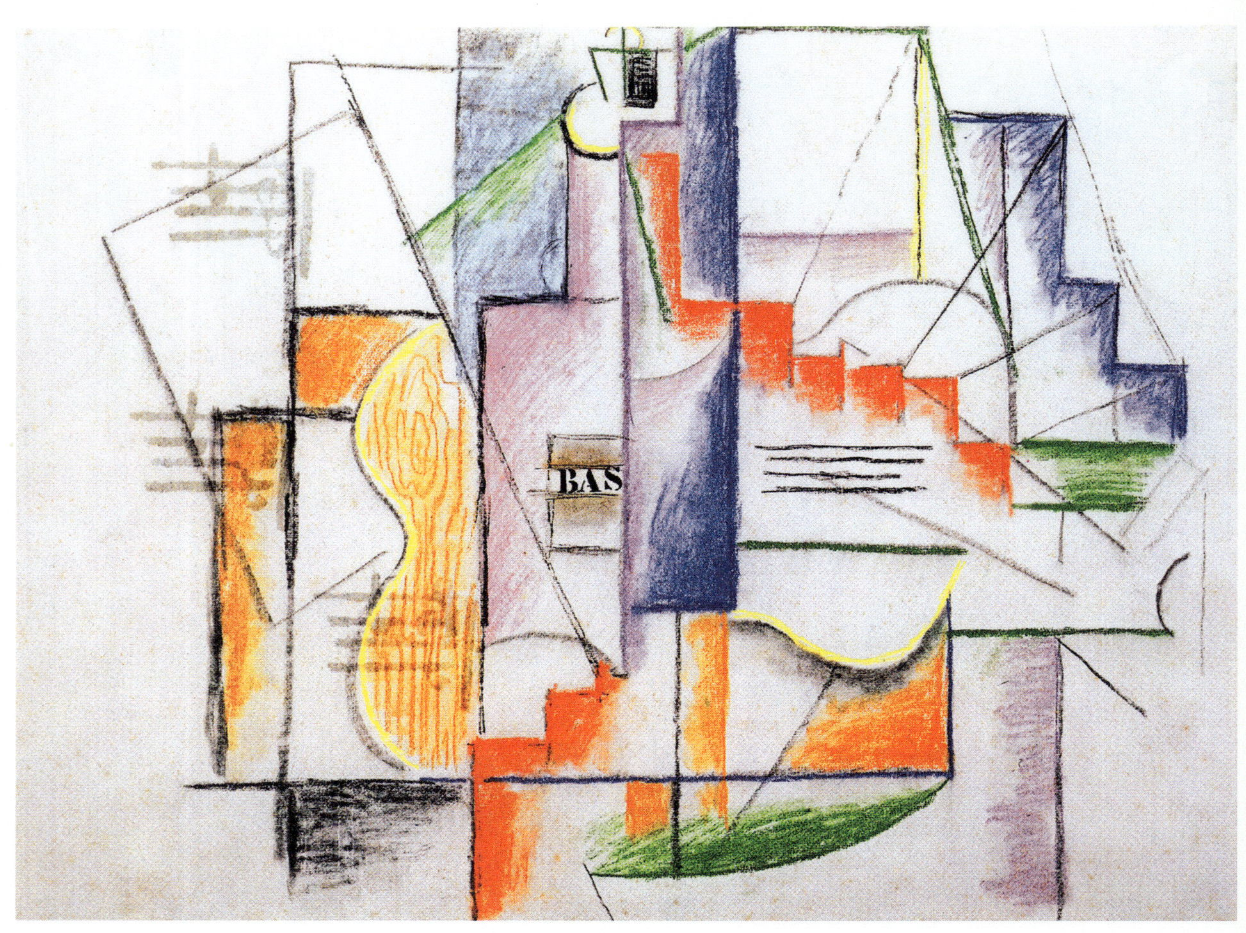

Pablo Picasso
(1881–1973)
BOTTLE OF BASS
AND GUITAR
20TH CENTURY
Pastel, charcoal,
and ink on paper
Private Collection/photo
Christie's Images/Bridgeman
Images © Succession Picasso/
DACS, London 2018

In Picasso's cubist work he often created still lifes of everyday objects such as musical instruments and glassware. His reasoning behind using these everyday objects was that he wanted to ensure any emotions felt from his work were a result of his style rather than from associations we might have with the subjects.

I want to tell something by means of the most common object.

PABLO PICASSO

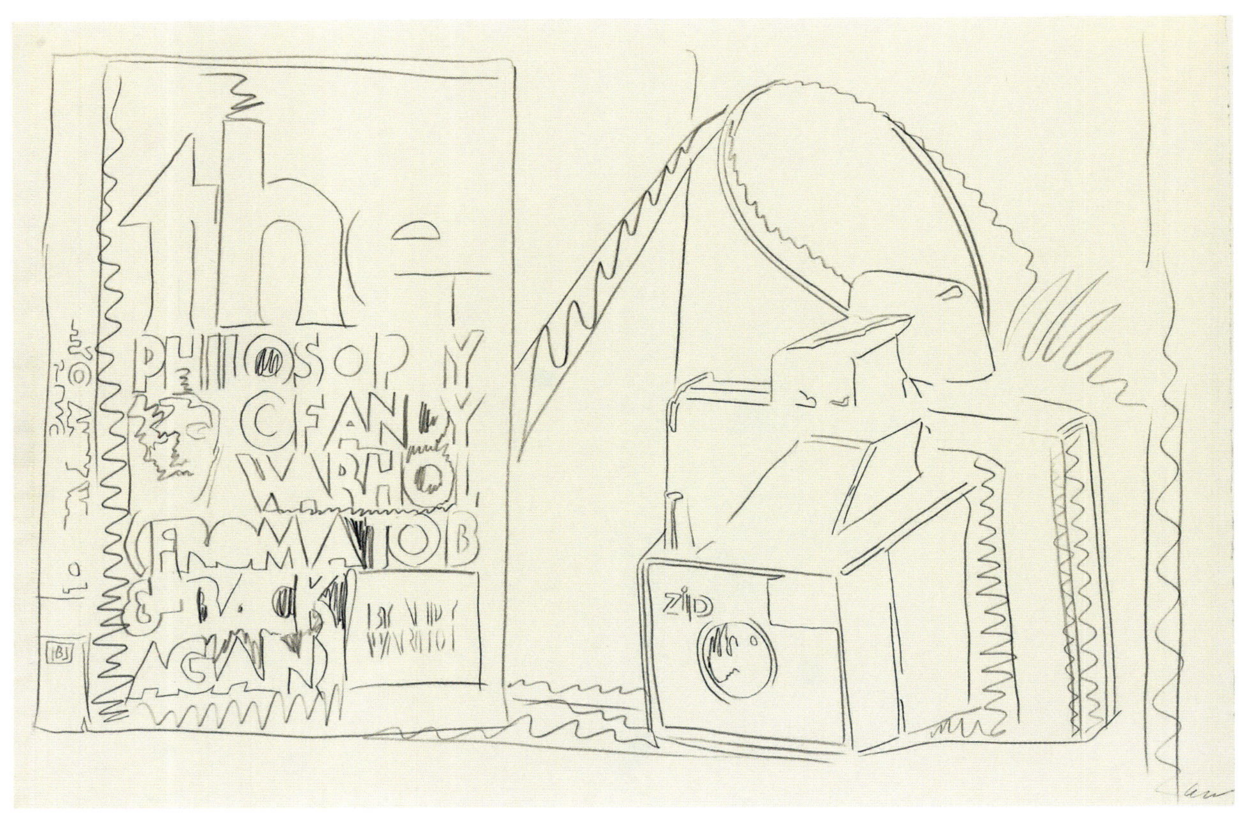the
PHILOSOPHY
OF ANDY
WARHOL
(FROM A TO B
& BACK
AGAIN)

You can find beauty in the simple objects available to you.
Their context, as well as their composition, is important.
Sometimes the power of the objects does not lie in what
they look like, but in what they mean to you personally.

Better to make a big thing out of a little subject
than to make a little thing out of a big one.
CHARLES WEBSTER HAWTHORNE

Hans Bol
(1534—1593)
DRAPED GARMENT
HANGING ON
TWO POINTS
1544–1593
Chalk on paper
Rijksmuseum, Amsterdam

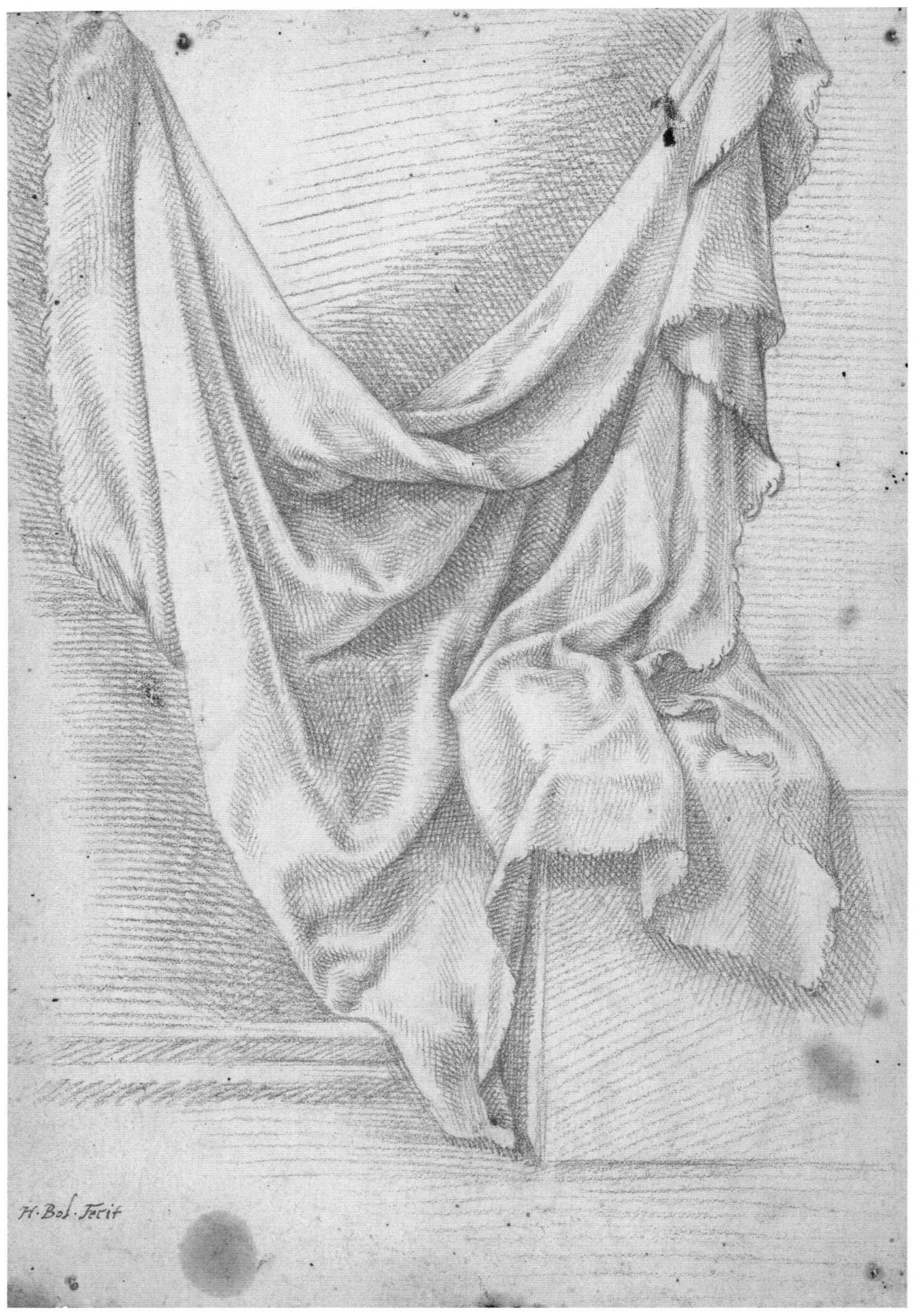

Drapery study was an important part of art training,
especially in fifteenth-century Italian workshops. This type
of formal study trains the artist to hone skills in showing
light and shadow to create an illusion of rippling cloth.

*Lines, always lines, and never body. But where do we see
these lines in nature? I see only forms which advance,
forms which recede, masses in light or in shadow.*
FRANCISCO DE GOYA

Georgia O'Keeffe
(1887–1986)
BANANA FLOWER
1934
Charcoal and black
chalk on paper
*The Museum of Modern Art,
New York/Scala, Florence
© Georgia O'Keeffe Museum/
DACS 2018*

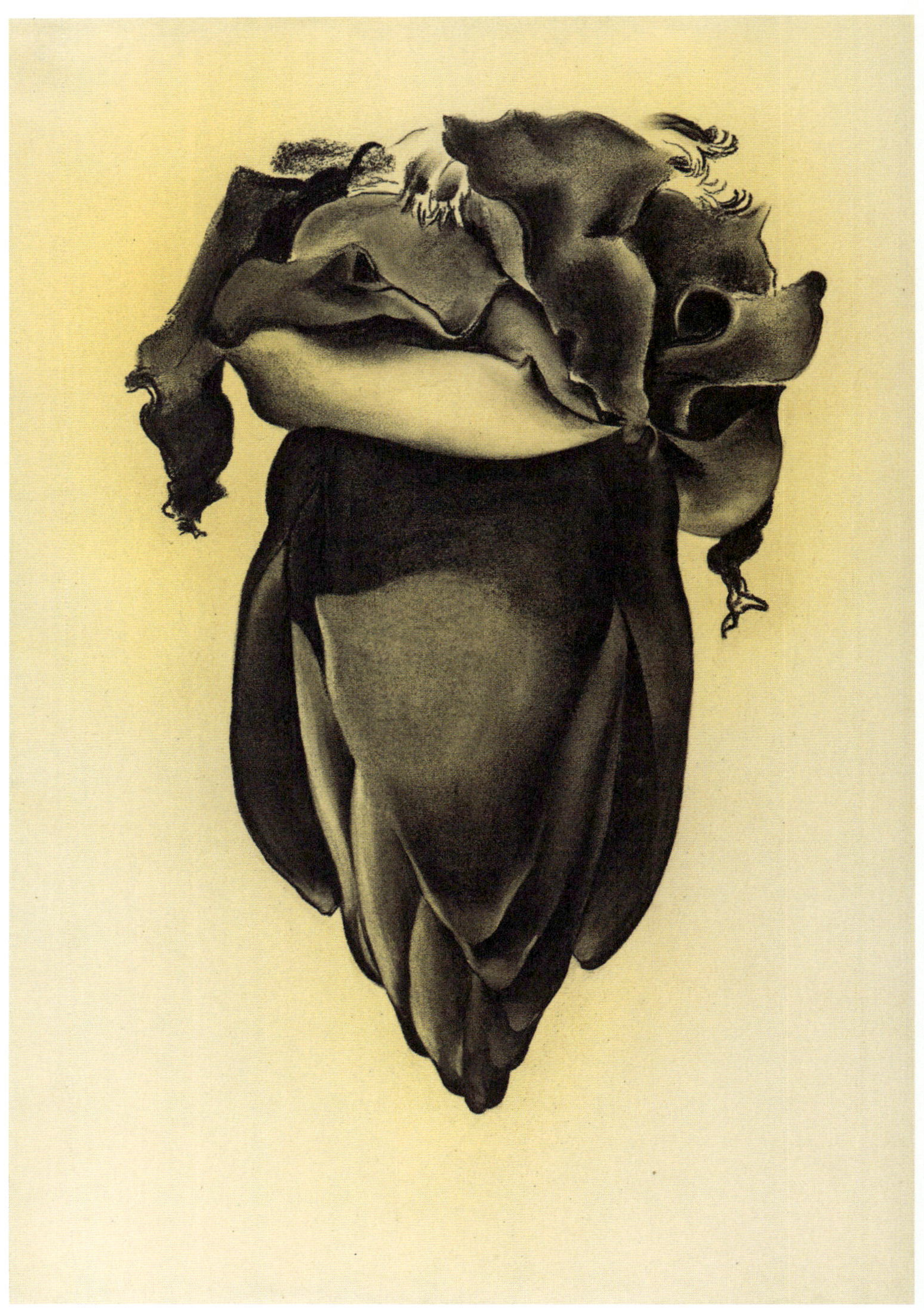

Charcoal does not allow kindness; it is sober, and only
with real emotion can you draw results from it.
ODILON REDON

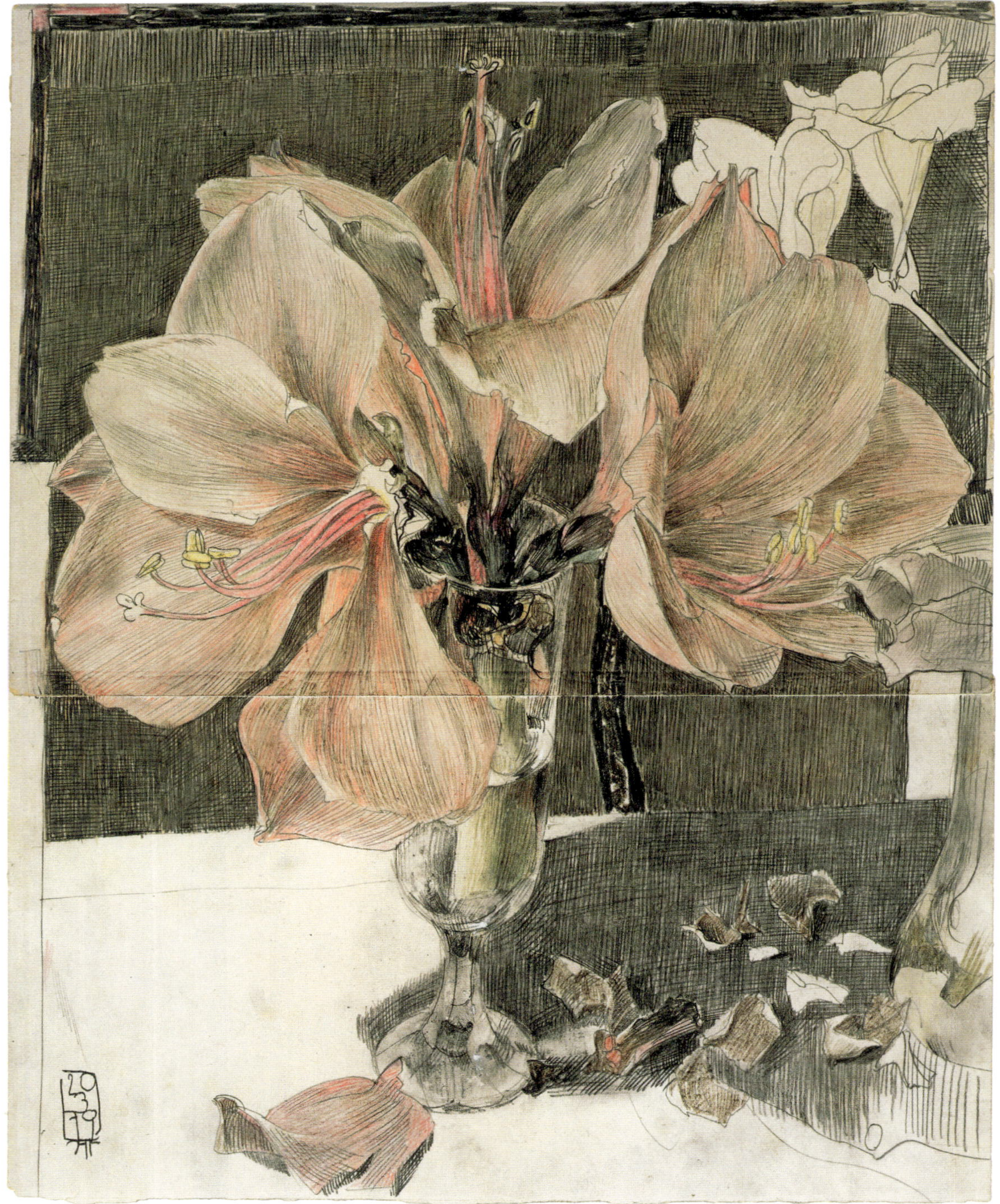

Horst Janssen
(1929–1995)
AMARYLLIS
1979
Pencil and color
pencil on paper

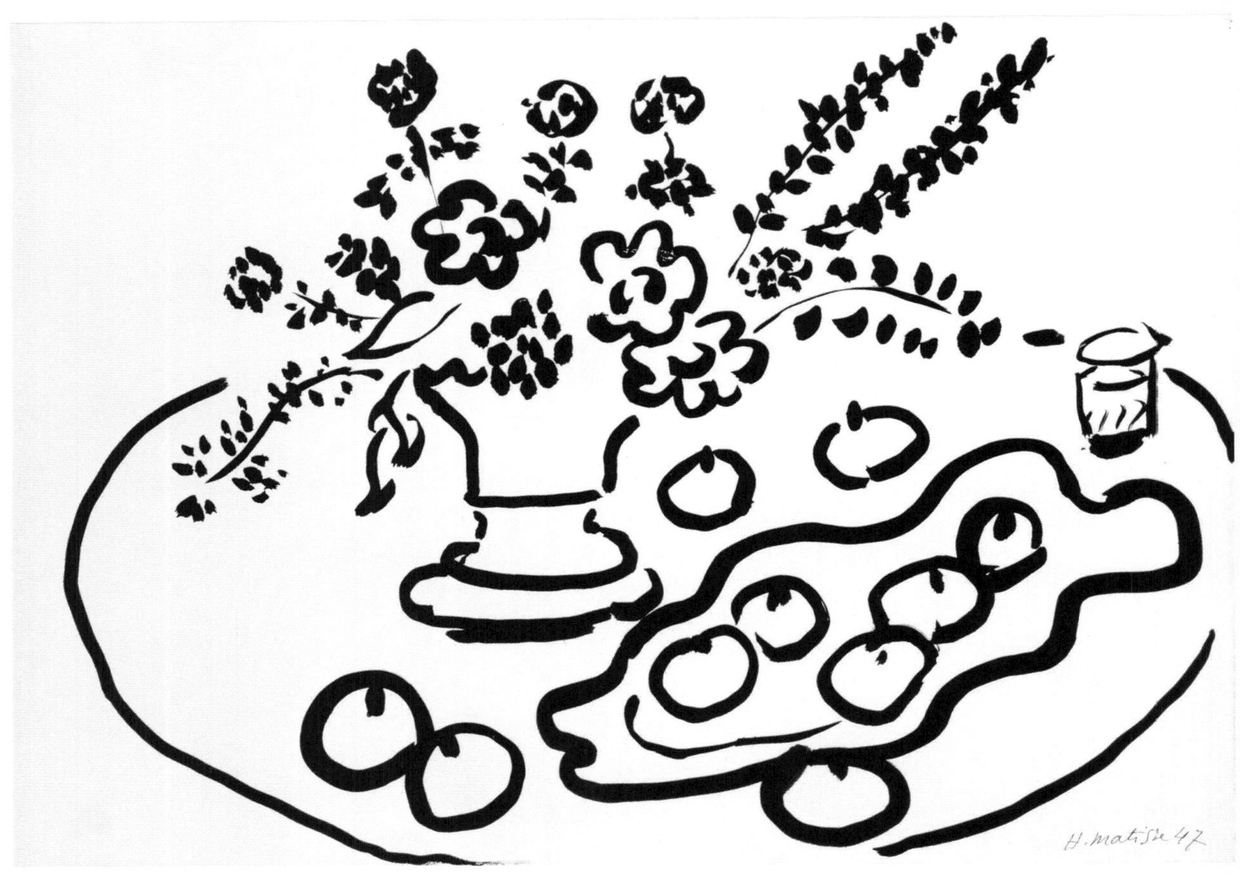

Henri Matisse
(1869–1954)
STILL LIFE
WITH VASE OF
FLOWERS AND
PLATE OF FRUIT
1947
Chinese ink on paper
*Museo d'Arte Moderna
di Ca' Pesaro, Venice/
Bridgeman Images
© Succession H. Matisse/
DACS 2018*

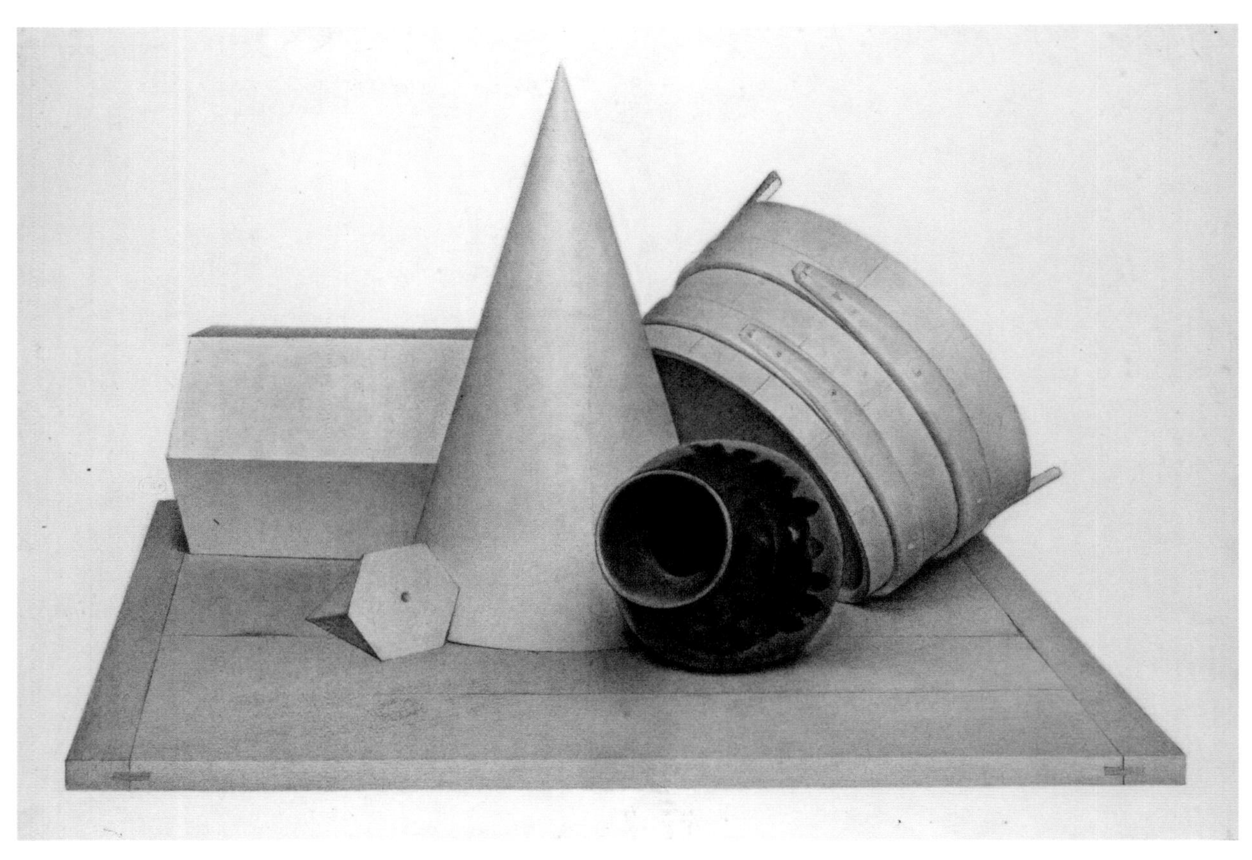

Walter Bonner Gash
(1869–1928)
STILL LIFE WITH
GEOMETRIC
MODELS AND
A VASE
20TH CENTURY
Soft pencil on paper
Private Collection © Liss Fine
Art/Bridgeman Images

This perfectly executed composition of objects is achieved by
beautifully precise and gentle shading with the softest of pencils.
The skillful blending renders any pencil stroke almost invisible.

Drawing is deception.
M. C. ESCHER

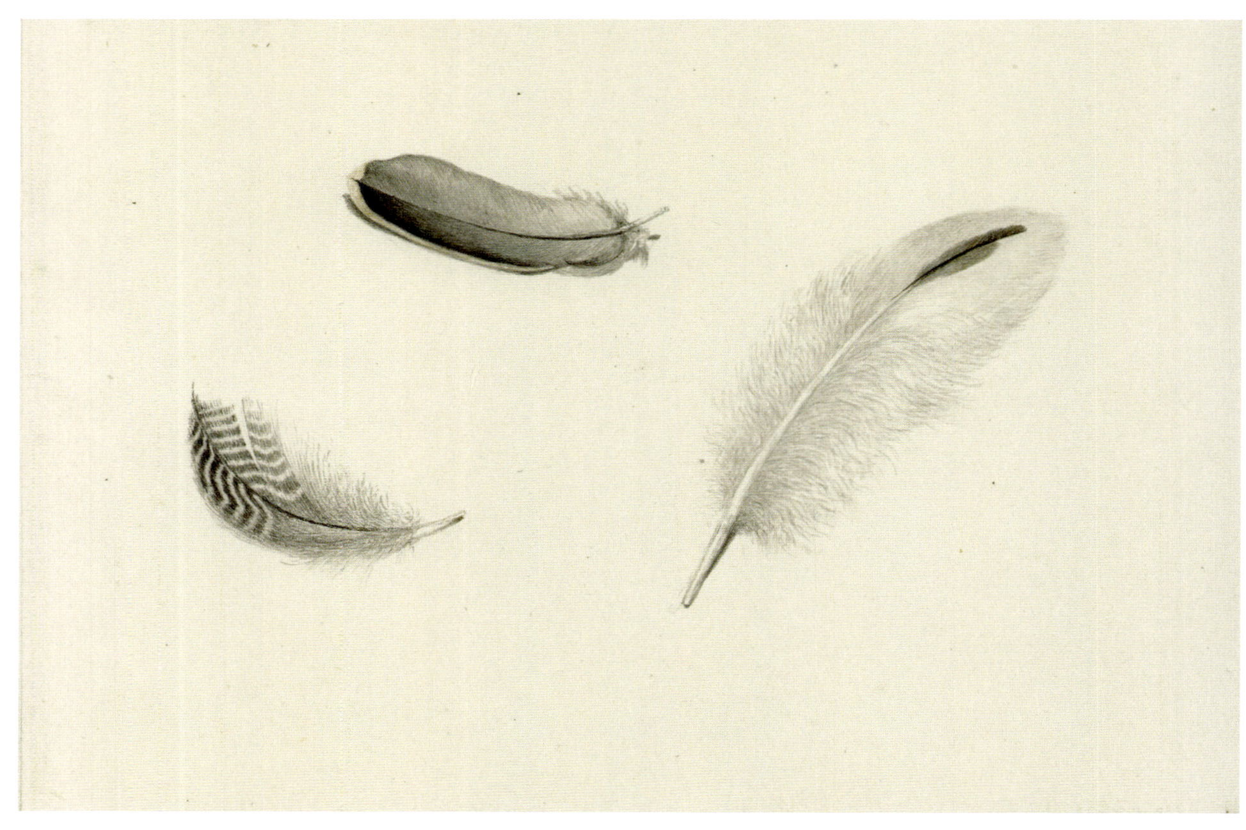

Dirk Salm
(1803–1838)
STUDY OF
THREE FEATHERS
1813–1838
Pencil, pen, and
ink on paper
Rijksmuseum, Amste-dam

The hair-breadth flicks that make up the feathers
here in Salm's drawing are built up so delicately
as to replace any sense of outline, and give the
feathers the look of complete weightlessness.

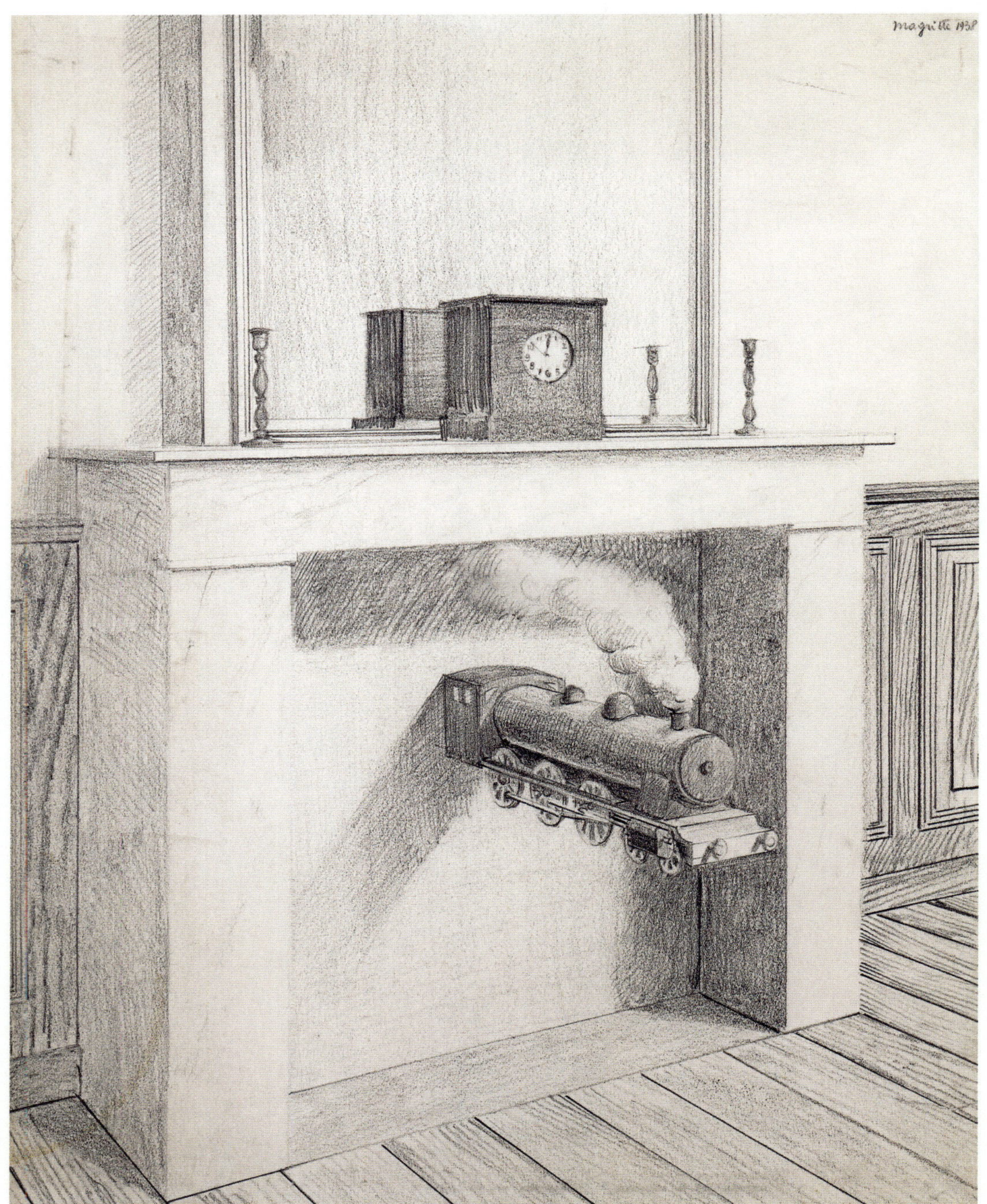

René Magritte
(1898–1967)
Time Transfixed
(La Durée
Poignardée)
1938
Pencil on paper

An object never performs the same function as its name or its image.
RENÉ MAGRITTE

*To be a surrealist . . . means barring from your mind
all remembrance of what you have seen, and being
always on the lookout for what has never been.*
RENÉ MAGRITTE

Roger de La Fresnaye
(1885–1925)
STILL LIFE
C.1920
Graphite, pen, and white
ink on brown paper
National Gallery of
Art, Washington.
Rosenwald Collection

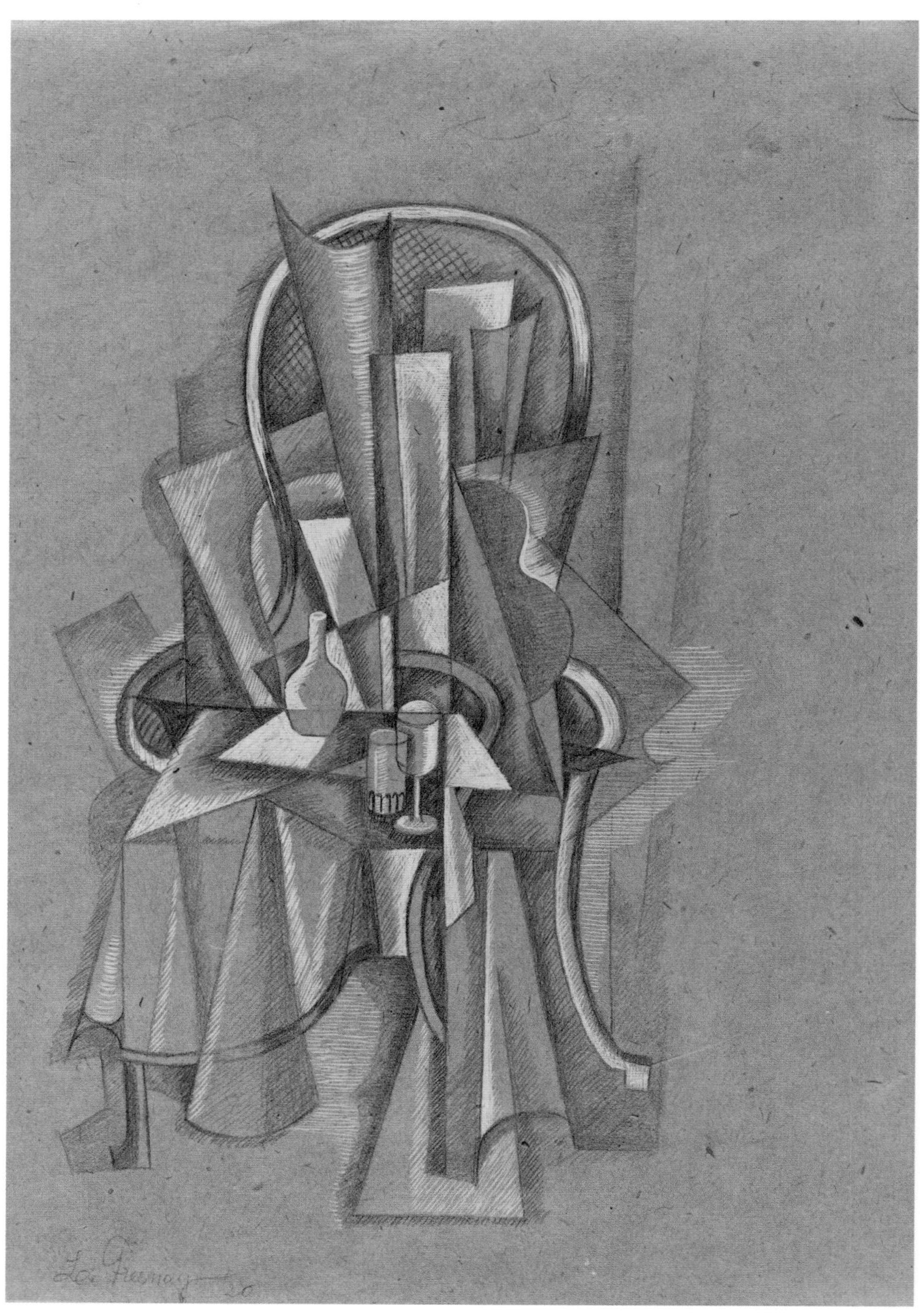

In this still life, the crisp quality of line strips the subjects of their
usual soft, rounded forms, and La Fresnaye furthers the stylized
geometric effect with a sensitive use of flat white color that
highlights and ties the fragmented shapes together.

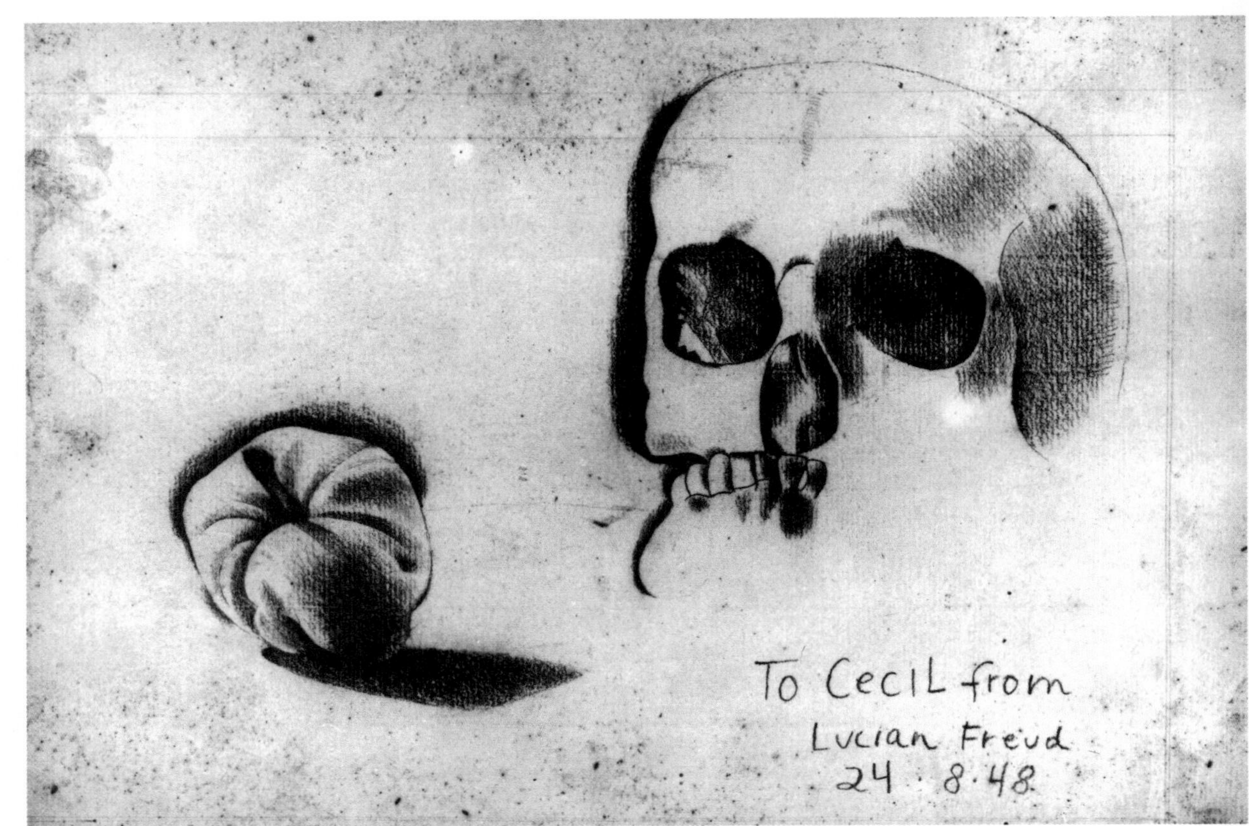

Lucian Freud
(1922—2011)
SKULL AND APPLE
1948
Charcoal on paper
Private Collection/
Bridgeman Images
© *The Lucian Freud Archive*

In this modern take on a traditional theme of mortality and the passing
of time, the decaying, temporary beauty of Freud's shrinking apple is
juxtaposed with the explicit placement of the skull to striking effect.

The skull has been a feature of artworks since Roman
times where it was a reminder of human mortality.
Images would also often be accompanied by the phrase
"omnia mors aequat" (death makes us equal).

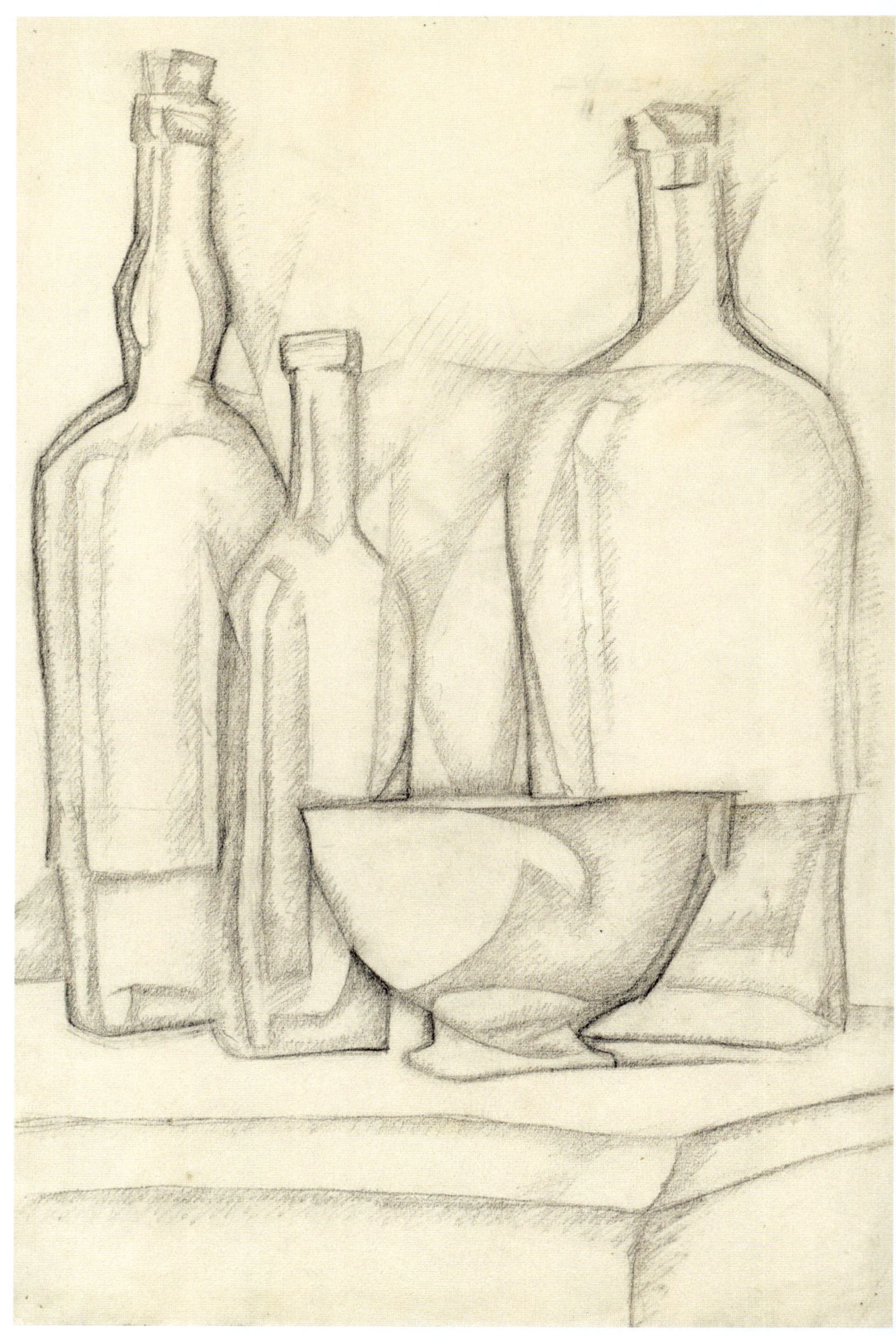

Juan Gris
(1887–1927)
BOTTLES
AND BOWL
1911
Graphite on laid paper
*National Gallery of Art,
Washington. Collection of
Mr. and Mrs. Paul Mellon*

Here Gris has reduced the composition to a flow of minimalist lines. Yet the objects, stripped to their most basic forms, become even more expressive as a result.

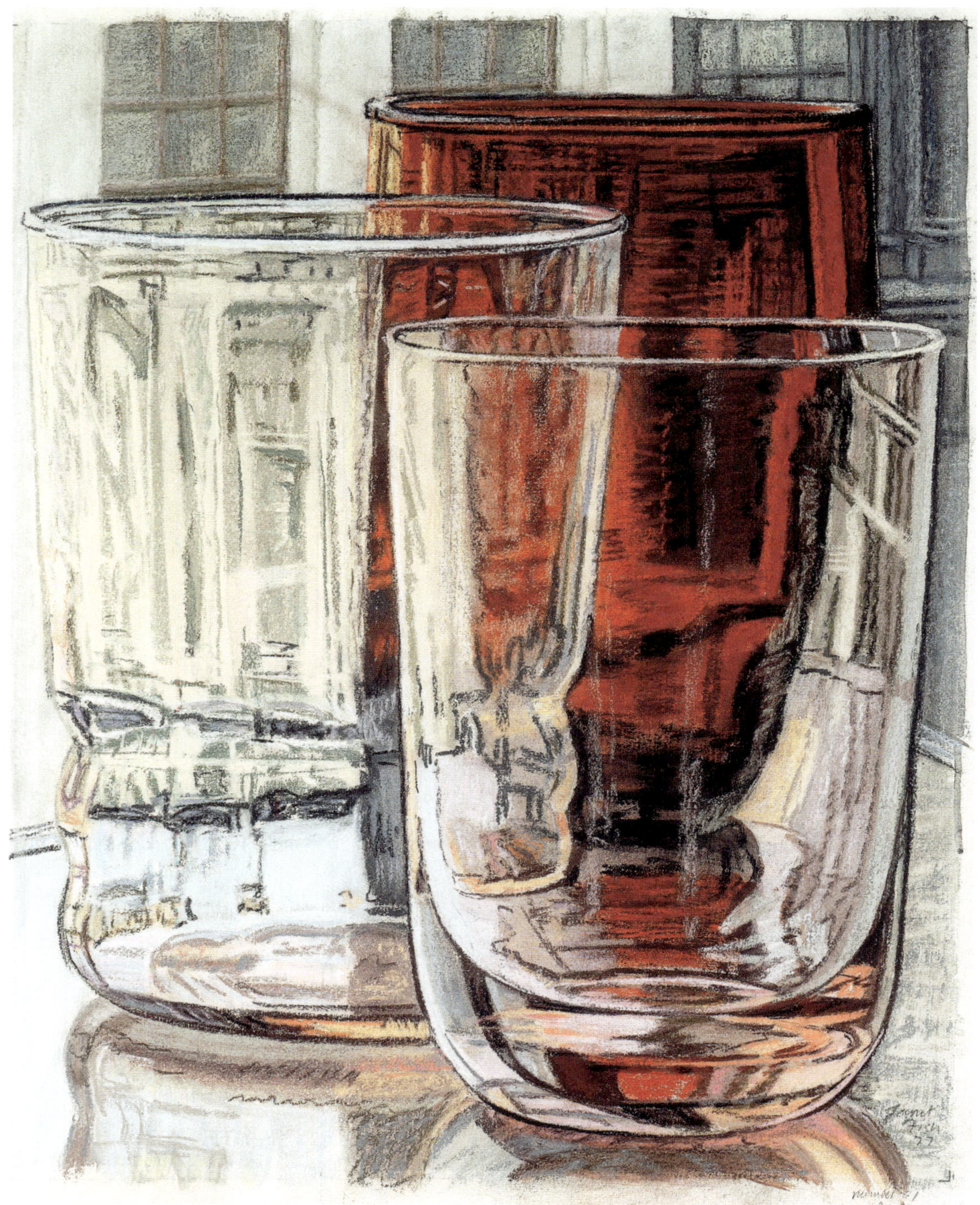

Janet Fish

(b.1938)

RED GLASSES

1977

Colored chalks on paper

Private Collection/photo Christie's Images/Bridgeman Images © Janet Fish. DACS, London/VAGA, New York 2018

Consider the behavior of light effects such as reflection
and refraction upon a shiny or transparent surface. Simplify
the object you are drawing and think purely in terms of light
and dark shapes. By drawing what you observe, even in
distortions, the drawing will come together coherently.

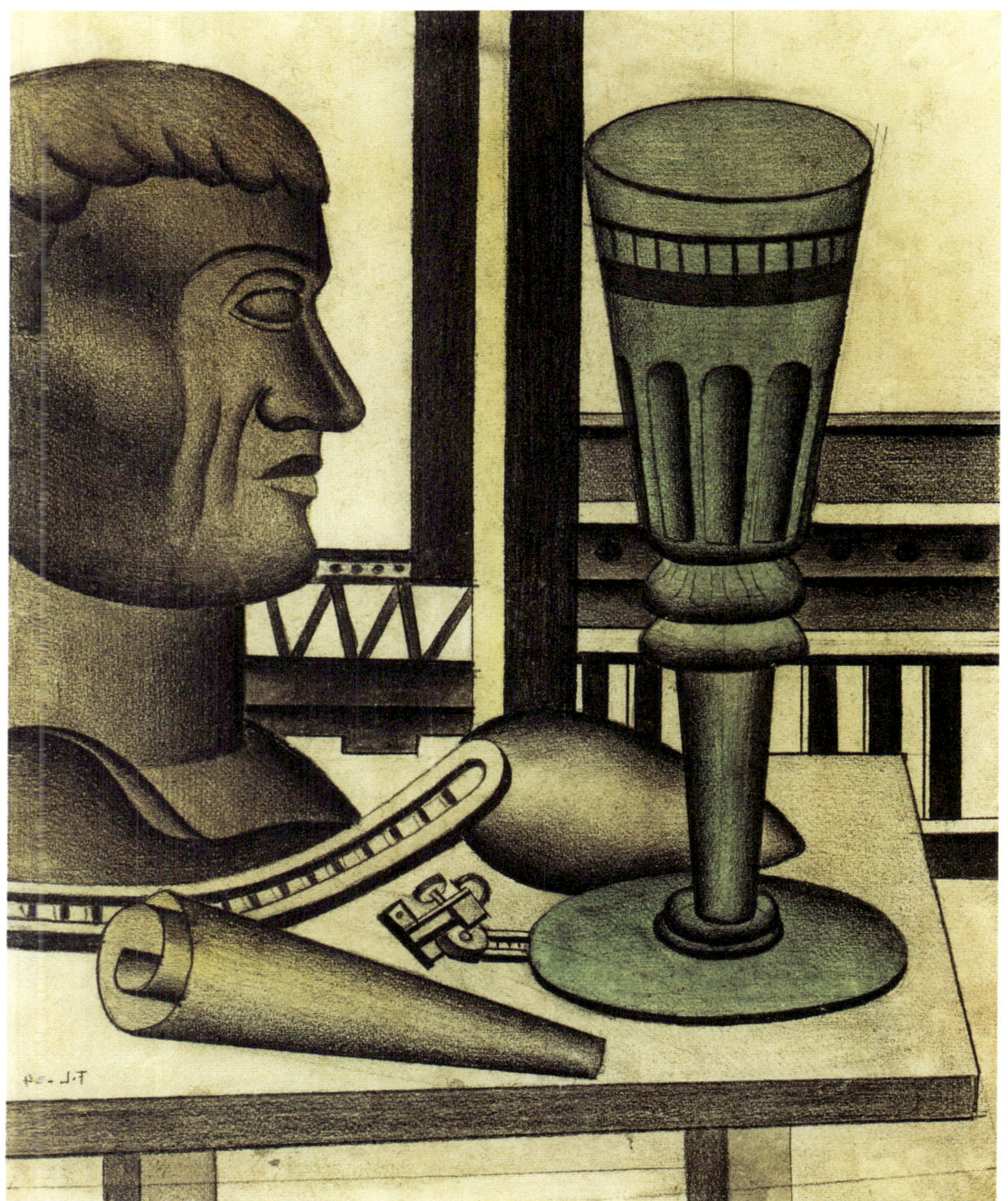

Fernand Léger
(1881–1955)
STILL-LIFE WITH
BUST (NATURE
MORTE AU BUSTE)
1924
Pencil, colored
pencils, and watercolor
on tan paper
*Private Collection/photo
Christie's Images/Bridgeman
Images © ADAGP, Paris and
DACS, London 2017*

Until we can insert a USB into our ear and download our thoughts,
drawing remains the best way of getting visual information on to the page.
GRAYSON PERRY

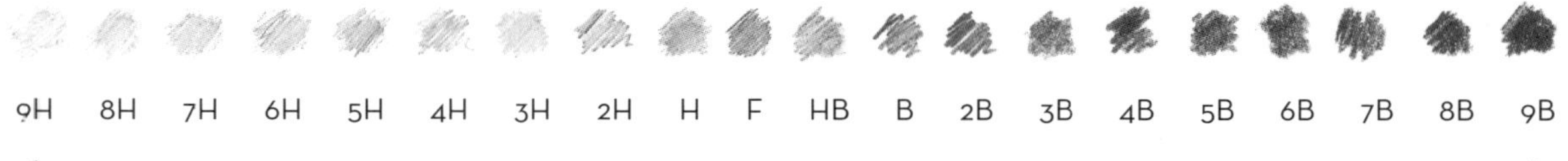

GRAPHITE OR LEAD PENCILS. These are graded from the hardest 9H (H for hard) up to the softest 9B (B for black), with HB (hard black) and F (fine) halfway in between. Soft pencils give a dense, black mark, while hard pencils give a gray mark. If you require a darker mark, do not apply more pressure, but switch to a softer pencil instead.

MECHANICAL PENCILS. These pencils can be extended as necessary without the need for constant sharpening.

WATER-SOLUBLE GRAPHITE PENCILS. These are available in a range of grades, and can be used dry, dipped in water, or the strokes worked into with a wet brush to create watercolor-like effects. They offer the versatility of combining linear marks with tonal washes.

GRAPHITE STICKS. Graphite sticks have a soft texture that makes them suited to large, bold drawings. Available in various sizes and grades, you can also buy them as irregular shaped chunks and as fine graphite powder that can be applied to textured paper.

CHARCOAL. This is the oldest drawing medium, dating from prehistoric times. It comes in different lengths and thicknesses, as well as chunks for especially expressive drawings. Stick charcoal, being brittle and powdery, is ideal for broad areas of tone. Compressed charcoal is made from charcoal dust and clay pressed into shape, and tends to be harder than stick charcoal, making it useful for more detailed, linear work. Charcoal pencils use compressed charcoal.

INKS. There are two main types of ink used by artists. Waterproof ink can be diluted with water and becomes permanent when dry, so line work can be overlaid with washes without smudging. Water-soluble ink, on the other hand, can be blended with water, or reworked with water when dry if corrections are needed.

DIP PENS AND NIBS. Nibs on dip pens can make lines of varying widths depending on the amount of pressure applied, or the back of the nib can be used to make broader marks. Dip pens do have to be reloaded with ink with each stroke, however, to get consistent marks.

SKETCHING PENS, FOUNTAIN PENS, AND TECHNICAL PENS. These are ideal sketching tools, enabling you to use ink on location without having to carry bottles of ink around.

ROLLERBALL, FIBER-TIP, AND MARKER PENS. These are good for sketching out ideas and come in a wide range of colors, but can lack variation in line width individually, although they are available in various sizes.

COLORED PENCILS. Colored pencils contain a colored pigment mixed with clay and coated with wax so that there is no need for a fixative when using them, as they do not smudge easily. Huge color ranges are available, but this is necessary as they cannot be physically blended together to create new shades.

WATER-SOLUBLE PENCILS. These can be used to make conventional pencil drawings but the strokes made with water-soluble pencils can also be worked into with water to create watercolor effects.

CONTÉ PENCILS AND CRAYONS. These are made from pigment and clay and are available either bound in wood to make pencils or as small square sticks. They are softer and less waxy than ordinary colored pencils, but not as soft and crumbly as pastels.

PASTELS. Pastels are exceptionally versatile and ideal for producing quick sketches where a bold effect is desired. They are available in hard and soft forms, but cannot be mixed physically to create new colors. Instead they have to be blended by overlapping strokes on the paper, hence there are many varieties of boxed sets in assorted colors.

OIL PASTELS. These pastels have an added binder of oil so they are not as crumbly as pure pastels and also smudge less. They have the thick, buttery quality of oil paints, and are good for bold, confident strokes. They respond like oil paints, and oil pastel drawings can be worked with a brush dipped in turpentine to achieve a wash effect or scratched into using a sgraffito technique.

PASTEL PENCILS. These have strong colors and the pencil shape makes them ideal for more detailed linear work.

PAPERS. The color, texture, and quality of the paper will play an important part in your finished picture. Dry media that is worked loosely and lightly will result in the color of the paper showing through. Pastels and charcoal will require a paper with enough texture to hold the powder, whereas conté pencils can be used on smoother grades of paper. The most common drawing paper has a smooth surface that is suitable for graphite, colored pencil, and ink work.

LARGE SOFT BRUSH. This is useful for brushing away excess dust when working with powdery media.

FIXATIVE. As charcoal, pastels, and other powdery media smudge easily, finished drawings made in these media should be sprayed with a fixative to bind the powder particles to the paper surface.

SHARPENER, SCALPEL, OR CRAFT KNIFE. These are needed to sharpen the points of pencils and pastel sticks.

TORCHON (stump of rolled paper). A torchon is useful for blending pastel colors and charcoal, though a rag or cotton swab will work too.

ERASERS. Kneaded or putty erasers are the most useful, as small pieces can be rolled off and shaped however you wish for subtle, precise erasing.

TECHNIQUES —

COLOR BLENDING. Use your finger, a torchon, a brush, or a piece of tissue to blend colors together smoothly on the paper.

SOFT BLENDING. This technique is ideally used with charcoal. As charcoal is a soft medium, you can blend it with your finger to create a smooth, velvety effect.

SCUMBLING. This is a term used to describe the technique of mixing colors optically by laying one color lightly over another. The area where the two colors overlap will give the illusion of a third color.

LINEAR STROKES. This technique is particularly useful for pastel sticks. Using a pastel stick on its widest side will achieve broad bands of color, running the tip or edge of the stick down the paper will produce thin lines, and using the flat end of the pastel will produce bands of color as thick as the pastel.

HATCHING. This is a technique where parallel lines are used to suggest tone and color. By varying the weight and density of the hatched lines, tonal variation can quickly be achieved to great effect. Looser, scribbled lines give a sketchier look.

CROSSHATCHING. This is a development of hatching to indicate differences in shade, where two or more sets of parallel lines are combined, one set crossing another at an angle. The lines can be crosshatched at any angle, or even curved to follow along shapes, and the density varied. However it is a labor-intensive technique.

POINTILLISM. This is a way of building up an area with small dots. By increasing the density of the dots you can increase the density of the color and shading effect. From a distance, dots that are more closely spaced will appear to merge in one mass of color even if they are not touching.

TONE. Tone is built up through a series of loose strokes. To practice, draw a small rectangle and fill it in slowly with strokes, increasing the density to achieve darker tones.

HIGHLIGHTS. These can be picked out in areas of tone by using a kneadable putty eraser or a stick of white chalk. Chalk will deliver sharper, cleaner highlights whereas a putty eraser is subtler.

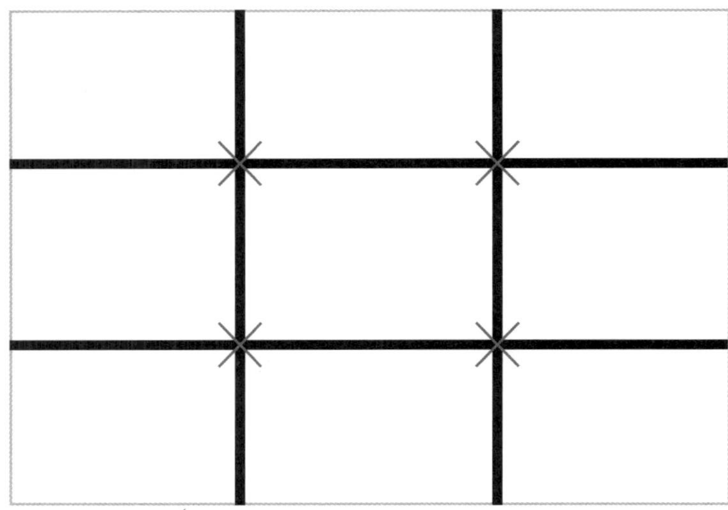

COMPOSITION, MEASURING, AND LIGHT —

COMPOSITION

Compositions for still lifes are endlessly flexible; as your subjects will not object, you can experiment with rearranging them until you are satisfied with how they look. Consider also that compositions need not necessarily be arranged; found objects can be equally pleasing in their natural and uncontrived placement. Aim to rid yourself of your preconceptions of each object, and consider the scene as a whole, distilling what you see into shapes, tones, and textures. You might want to try making a viewfinder by cutting out a rectangle from a piece of card to make a frame that you can move around, to see how an image would look framed from different angles, and in a portrait or landscape orientation. The rule of thirds is also a helpful starting point; it is an artistic device whereby you divide your paper into three equal sections horizontally and vertically—placing your objects at one of the intersections should result in a more interesting and balanced composition.

MEASURING

Even the most proficient artist needs to continually check while working that all the proportions drawn are true to life. When drawing a still-life scene, close one eye and holding a pencil at arm's length, measure, for example, the distance from the top to the bottom of the arrangement, using the tip of your thumb against the pencil as your measurement mark. Transfer this unit of measurement to the paper

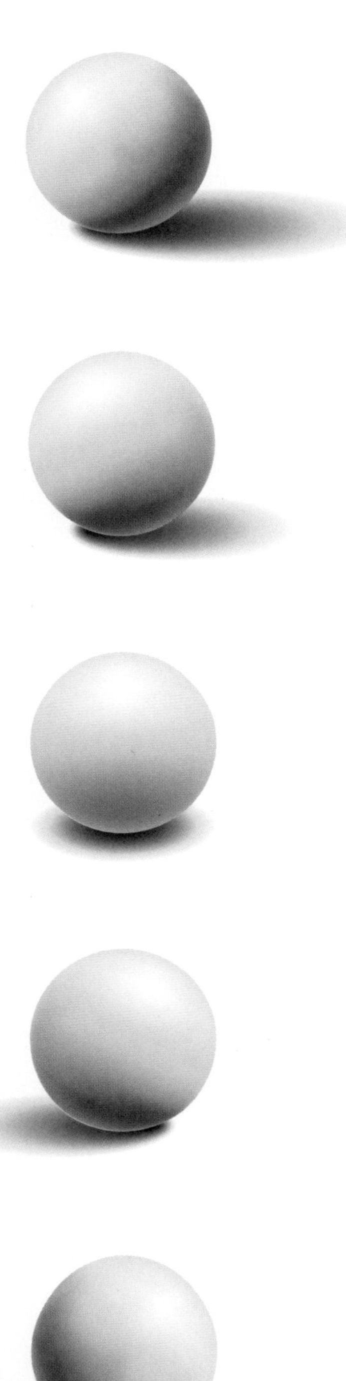

relative to the scale you are drawing to, for example drawing at double the size of the pencil measurements. You can then use this same scale to measure the distances of all the objects, so that the ratio will be consistent when applied to the paper. You can also measure the negative spaces between and around your objects—as negative spaces are abstract shapes you will be more inclined to draw what you see rather than what you know, and build up a more accurate drawing.

This is one of the most common pitfalls for the beginner, as objects closer to the eye appear larger than those further away. When tackling a foreshortened object, it is important to rely on measurements and observations, and use the background to map the various points where the object meets it. A good technique to practice foreshortening is to work from a photograph: draw a grid over the photograph and also over your paper to accurately scale up the outline of the object in the photograph and enlarge it to your drawing. You can use the gridlines to measure from and achieve the right ratio, then draw or paint on top of the plotted outline.

LIGHT

How the light falls in an arrangement will affect the mood in a drawing. A softer light, such as light from a north-facing window or from a cloudy day, will produce less defined shadows. Harsher light, such as from direct sunlight or hard overhead lighting, will result in more dramatic contrasts where shadows form new shapes around the objects and highlights are much clearer. It's useful to remember that artificial light is consistent and means you can return to the arrangement as many times as you wish, or draw for as long as you like, whereas daylight will change throughout a day. The angle of the light source will also affect where shadows and highlights fall, as well as how big the shadows are—if the light source is near horizontal compared to the object, the shadow will be very long in the opposite direction and if the light source is directly overhead, the shadow will be directly underneath.

the STILL-LIFE
SKETCHBOOK

Line, shape, space, composition, and depth are most easily understood through the study and practice of still-life drawing. The artist can enjoy the freedom of arranging objects exactly as desired, testing perception, and pushing the boundaries of reality.

Take inspiration from the words and works of 20 great still-life artists, including the fantastically detailed works of the sixteenth-century Dutch masters, through to the cubist and surreal compositions of Picasso and O'Keeffe.

Two Apples, by Édouard Manet,
National Gallery of Art, Washington.
Collection of Mr. and Mrs. Paul Mellon

£12.99 UK / $12.99 US / $14.99 CAN

ISBN 978-1-78157-534-5

9 781781 575345

www.ilex.press

ilex